Shame on You ... No More

Shame on You ... No More

A Worship Leader's Journey

Cathy Little

abbott press®

A DIVISION OF WRITER'S DIGEST

Shame on You ... No More
A Worship Leader's Journey

Unless otherwise identified, all Scripture quotations are from
the Holy Bible, New International Version (NIV) Copyright
©1973, 1978, 1984, 2011 by Biblica.Inc™.

Abbott Press books may be ordered through booksellers or by contacting:

Abbott Press
1663 Liberty Drive
Bloomington, IN 47403
www.abbottpress.com
Phone: 1-866-697-5310

ISBN: 978-1-4582-0035-8 (e)
ISBN: 978-1-4582-0036-5 (sc)

Library of Congress Control Number: 2011914584

Printed in the United States of America

Abbott Press rev. date: 8/25/2011

To Diane,
Who walked the hard road with me
but always looked
beyond my behavior and
saw my potential.
and

To Charlotte,
Who persistently validated me,
loved me,
challenged me
and encouraged me to share my story.
In loving memory:
April 5, 1951-December 2, 2007

ACKNOWLEDGEMENTS

The players on this stage and the companions on this journey have been far too numerous to list individually. Who I am today is the sum total of a myriad of influences, and I am grateful to all of them for playing their roles.

Thank you to Sarah, for planting the first seed that I should write a book; to Kim and Rebekah for providing me that incredible first opportunity to share my story; to Danny and Debi for speaking prophetically to me with words that drew me closer to my destiny; to Charlotte for never being shocked, for always pressing in and for being so absolutely consistent; to Diane, for being Jesus to me no matter how difficult I made it, for never giving up on me when I ran or pushed, for always believing in me and for continually speaking the truth in love; to everyone who spoke the truth to me even when I could not receive it; and to my mom and dad for loving me the best they knew how, for providing me with a Christian foundation, and for always supporting me. I love you all dearly.

Thank you to all who have provided input, critiques and proofing for this project along the way. Thank you especially to Claire, my sister, my friend and confidant, for her amazing photography, illustrations and artistic bent in this venture.

Above all, thank you to the One who knows me the best and loves me the most, the One who has relentlessly pursued me from before time began, my Father God. "Your love has captivated my heart, Your grace has found the deepest places, Your mercy has drawn me to Your side, and I will not be moved."

PREFACE

The following is my account of various events and circumstances in my life. The stories and illustrations are presented from my personal perspective. I don't believe that everyone intentionally sets out to shame another. What I do believe, however, is that wounded people wound others.

Although things that were said or done to me along my journey affected me negatively, I do not believe that anyone referred to in this book *meant* to do me harm, nor do I hold anything against them. My heart has grown from resentment to compassion as I realize that the world is full of broken, wounded people who often do not receive the tools to love each other as God intended. Many of them are simply passing along the dysfunction to which they were accustomed.

I do not wish away the wounds of my past, for without them, I would not be who I am today. The point is to acknowledge them, learn from them, forgive and move on. My prayer is that my story will help the reader find his or her own way into the freedom that God intended.

CONTENTS

THE INTRODUCTION

Just write the book ... stop thinking about it and just write the book.

This was not my idea. I distinctly remember a conversation I had with a friend after returning from a women's retreat with a church in southwest Florida. I had been asked along with another friend to lead worship during the weekend, which we had done together many times, but this time I was also asked to share my story. I spoke during the final session of the retreat and was amazed as I watched God take the stuff of my life and use it to bring healing and restoration to those who were there.

I had the opportunity to pray over many of those women and I saw God begin to break chains and bring freedom and healing right in front of my eyes. It blew me away.

In sharing with my friend about all of what God had done through my vulnerability and the telling of my story, she blurted out, "You should write a book". I laughed, but from that moment on, I could not get the idea out of my head. Her words were confirmed to me on several levels and I came to know in my heart that God had not only called me to write this book, but He had commissioned me with the authority to do so.

I began writing in the weeks following, but nothing took shape. I was overwhelmed by the task before me and I had no real direction. After a brief attempt, and a major life-altering event, I quit writing altogether.

Although I never lost the idea of the book and I knew it would get written eventually, it was more than a year later that God began to reawaken the importance of His call. I began to ask people around me to pray that he would give me all that I needed to step into the task, but ultimately I knew I just needed to start writing.

Just write the book! It sounds much easier than it is. I have heard it said that an author cannot write and edit at the same time. You just have to throw it all up and get it out there. Editing comes later. But, I am an editor. I can't just put it out there without crafting it perfectly and making it a bestseller right out of the starting gate. What if I fail? What if I look badly? What if people don't like it? What if it's not good enough? What if I don't measure up? What if I say too much? What if I say too little? What if … ?

As I reflect on my life, I realize that I have always been an editor. I have not been an editor in the common sense of editing words, but I have been a master editor of me. I have always been quick to edit myself so as not to offend anyone, in order to impress someone or simply so that I do not fail. I have edited my behavior, I have edited my performance, I have edited my appearance, and I have edited my reactions. I am an editor. And somewhere in the shuffle, I lost my true self. Perhaps I never knew who I was to begin with.

I spent most of my life adjusting, compensating, modifying and editing, being afraid of failing, disappointing someone or not being good enough. As a result, I lost a sense of who I truly was. I lived in a continual cycle of being wounded, and ultimately, it was exhausting to be me.

My value was often connected to and qualified by how well I performed, how appropriately I dressed, how much I conformed to the standard (whatever it was on a given day), to who liked me, to who my friends were ... or weren't, on how well I behaved, etc. I was always searching for the ever illusive, "good job", or "way to go" because somewhere along the way, I had received a message that I was defined by what I did and that my value and acceptance were based on how well I did it. I was a human-*doing* rather than a human-*being* ... or at least that's how I operated.

I am the youngest of six children, and I was not expected, planned or even wanted necessarily. My parents started out wanting only two children, but ended up with six. They were done after child number five, and for six years they thought the family was complete. But then, surprise! Number six was on the way. People usually get a laugh out of the fact that my mother thought she had food poisoning when it was actually me! True story. I was definitely not planned.

3

The scales tipped just a bit and the family equilibrium was disrupted when I came onto the scene. My dad was a physician who lived a lifestyle of burying himself in his career and my mother was basically raising the family on her own. With five children already ages 6 to 13 needing to be driven in five different directions at five different times, I felt a bit lost in the shuffle. My sister who is 10 years older than me claims that I was her first child because she pretty much raised me. My mom was simply overloaded.

From what I have been told, I spent a great deal of effort during those first few years screaming (literally) for attention. My sister loves to remind me that she used to hold me in her lap in a hammerlock while I threw temper tantrums. Eventually I would give up and fall asleep in her arms.

Looking back, I can see that I spent a great deal of energy screaming for attention. Although my methods changed over the years, I still fought for it. I just wanted to feel loved. I wanted to be noticed. I was searching for acceptance and value. It often felt illusive to me, as if I was only the sum total of my performance, but I was never good enough.

I grew up in the church and was introduced very early to the idea that God loved me. I sang songs like, "Jesus loves me, this I know, for the Bible tells me so", and I memorized John 3:16, yet unfortunately, the message of God loving me was often coupled with an ever morphing and often impossible to master list of do's and don'ts. Even God's love and acceptance seemed illusive and always just out of my reach. I could never measure up.

As I have had opportunities to share my story, I am finding more and more that what has plagued me for most of my life is actually a very common battle. It may manifest itself in varying degrees and look a bit differently on different people, but the problem itself is almost universal. It is amazing to me how many people share my struggle, when all along I felt as if I were alone. This is my story. My prayer for you, the reader, is that God will touch you through it and bring you into the freedom He created you to have.

THE PROBLEM

After years of striving, many damaged relationships, jumping through hoops, living in fear, self-hatred and wasted energy, someone finally put words on my struggle. Someone put a key in the lock and chains that bound me my entire life started to fall off. Layers of the onion began to peel away and it was as if a veil was lifted from my eyes. I began a journey into the freedom God had always intended for me to have.

In the summer of 2002, I attended a conference in Augusta, GA. The conference was a three-day, bi-annual event for pastors and leaders in the southeast region of Vineyard churches. It was an opportunity to build community between leaders, and also to provide encouragement and training. I had been volunteering at my church and operating in various leadership roles for several months, so my pastor thought it would be good for me to participate and to learn more about the Vineyard in general, and to become better equipped and trained as a leader.

Most of the breakout sessions did not look interesting or feel appropriate to me, but one caught my eye. It was a two-part session held back to back during the second afternoon of the conference. I was drawn to it. Something intrigued me about the title. I had to go. It felt important.

No one in the room looked familiar to me, but it struck me that the space was filled to capacity. Some people were standing along the back wall. Some were sitting on the floor. Every chair was occupied. This was a room filled with pastors and leaders. Is it possible that they all needed to be here? Was this a topic that applied to *them*?

As the speaker began, it was as if light bulbs started to go off all around. It was a huge 'ah-ha' moment for me. There were words for my struggle. There were other people battling the same thing that I was battling. There were answers, and most importantly, there was hope!

The breakout session was called, *"Wounded by Shame, Healed by Grace"*. Shame … "Shame on you!" "You're such a screw up!" "You are such a disappointment, a failure," "You're not good enough." Shame … This was it! This had been my battle. This is what had plagued me my entire life.

In his book, "Tired of Trying to Measure Up," author Jeff VanVonderan talks about the difference between shame and guilt. Often they are used interchangeably, he says, but they are not. Shame is not guilt, and guilt is not shame. Guilt is based on behavior and it accompanies a sense of responsibility for a wrongdoing.

Since it is based on a behavior, you can fix the guilt by changing the behavior. If you feel guilty about lying, then tell the truth. If you feel guilty about hitting your sister, then stop hitting her. Repent, ask forgiveness and turn from the behavior. Guilt is a God-given prompting that perhaps you should re-think your choice of action or change your conduct.

Shame, however, is much more difficult to fix. Shame is a belief that you hold about yourself as a person. Shame says you are not good enough. Shame says you are unworthy, you are unlovable and that there is something wrong with you.[1]

Shame is not the result of a behavior, it is the way you view and define yourself. Changing your behavior will never fix the shame you feel because it is deeply rooted in the perceived fact that you are somehow defective, unlovable, invaluable and ultimately worthless. The antonym, or opposite of shame is self-esteem or self-respect, so in essence, shame is the absence of self-esteem and self-respect.

Whereas guilt causes us to feel badly for **doing** something wrong, we feel shame for **being** something wrong, according to VanVonderan.

I spent a great deal of energy trying to behave and perform. I poured all that I had into getting straight A's. I did everything I could to avoid mistakes, to look the part, to somehow feel like I measured up—to feel valued, accepted and loved. But behaving well could never fix my struggle with shame. It just made me tired.

---

1 Jeff VanVonderan, *Tired of Trying to Measure Up*, (Bethany House Publishers, 1989), 16

VanVonderan puts words on many of the specifics of the battle with shame. I ordered his book immediately after returning from the conference and when it arrived in the mail a few days later, I sat mesmerized by what I was reading.

I could not put the book down. I was captivated as I read page after page of what could have easily been my own life story. The book is written in two parts, the first deals with shame, and the second deals with God's love and grace. I read the first half of the book in one sitting. I could not stop. Someone had finally figured me out! For the first time in my life, I began to have a frame of reference for understanding me!

It is not my intention to re-write VanVonderan's book, but I do, however, use it as a reference point for much of what you will read in the next few chapters. My story is woven into and around the nuts and bolts of the struggle with shame. I only use his points as a springboard into my own journey. I do highly recommend that you pick up a copy and read it as well, for it will provide much more detailed information.

THE MESSAGE

Every child comes into this world with three basic needs, according to VanVonderan. He or she needs to feel loved and accepted with no strings attached. He or she needs to feel valued. And he or she needs to know that he or she belongs, that he or she is not alone. These are basic needs, and they come with the package of being human.

Unfortunately, somewhere along the way, we can get the message that we are not loved and accepted, and that we don't belong. We begin to believe that we somehow do not quite measure up.

There is an old saying that proclaims, "No man is an island". How true that statement is. VanVonderan talks about how we are all a part of various systems in our lives. We are members of different groups of people that are all related to each other and are dependent on each other in some way.

The family unit is an example of a system. Each member of the family is related to the other and in some way dependent on the other. The same goes for a church, school, sports team or work place … you get the idea. These are all groups of people in different settings that interact with and depend on each other.

In every system, the members affect and impact the other members. Messages are given and received both verbally and non-verbally that can communicate love, value and acceptance, or they can withhold it. Some messages will breathe life into the other members of the system. And unfortunately, some can knock the wind out of your sails and communicate shame—"You're not good enough" … "You don't measure up". These systems are built in and on shame.

Some of the messages that come from this type of system are blatantly shaming. Some are not quite as obvious. Regardless of the delivery, the point is made and the damage is done.

Have you ever been told, "Shame on you!" or "What is *wrong* with you?" Perhaps you have even said those words to someone else. The message can't be more blatant than that. These words communicate that there is something *wrong* with you. When you are told that you are stupid, or that you're a failure or a disappointment, eventually these messages take root. If you're told something long enough, even if it isn't true, sooner or later it will become your reality. You will begin to believe that you really are a failure. You will begin to be hooked by shame.

Shaming messages can be communicated in many different shapes and forms, says VanVonderan, but their impact is sure nevertheless. Sometimes the messenger of shame is when acceptance is given or withheld based on your performance. If the only way to get approval is to bring home straight "A's" on your report card, to get that big account, or to win that contest—not come in second or even tie for first, but to actually win it, then you begin to believe that you are only as good as the results you produce.

There were several times when I was growing up when I would be asked to do some household chore, and I would do it the best I knew how. But, when I told my mom that I was finished, she never seemed to approve of the job I had done. I had always missed a spot or forgotten a particular step. There were certain ways that things needed to be done, and there was never room for a different opinion or perspective. If it wasn't done the way my mom would have done it, then it was incorrect. I often received the message that I did not measure up because I had not done the project the way my mom thought it should be done. I didn't get the approval and acceptance I was seeking until I had done it up to her standards.

Another way shaming messages are communicated is an environment where you are surrounded by unspoken rules. You know the kind—the rules you don't know are there until you break them.

In his book, Jeff VanVonderan talks about two common "unspoken rules". The first is the "can't talk" rule. This is when pointing out a problem ends up making you the problem.

For example, I know of a pastor who was accused on more than one occasion of inappropriate conduct. A church staff member felt that the indiscretions needed to be brought out into the light because as a pastor, this behavior could not be allowed to go on. He decided to expose the activity and in turn was shamed and slandered for bringing it up. He became the problem because he exposed the problem. The attention was shifted off of the pastor who was caught in sin and onto the one who broke the "can't talk" rule.

VanVonderan points out that in addition to the "can't talk" rule, there is also the "can't win" rule. This is the rule that is made up of two parts and it is impossible to abide by one half without breaking the other. This puts you into a position where you simply cannot win. It is a set up for failure, and the message that you are not ok. "Always tell the truth and be honest, and don't tell your Aunt Edna that you don't like her cherry pie." Which is it?

I attended a Christian school for all of my twelve years. The two oldest siblings in my family had already graduated when this new school opened, but the remaining four of us transferred in when I was entering the first grade. My sisters were in the 10th and 12th grades, and they both participated in a singing group that the school had. When my brother got into the senior high, he too participated. It was a dream of mine to follow in their footsteps and also be a part of this "by audition only" team that got to travel to different churches and to compete with other schools.

When I finally reached my sophomore year, I auditioned for the team and I made it! I loved it but between my sophomore and junior years, the director of the ensemble left and another took his place. No longer was the group by audition only, but with the new director came some big changes. In order to be in the group, you now had to sign a behavior and dress code contract.

There were things I was being asked to sign a commitment to that I could not in good conscience commit to. I had been taught to be honest. I had been told to be true to my word so I could not sign my name to something I did not agree with and knew I would not abide by.

By not signing the contract, I was breaking the "can't win" rule that said, "Always be honest and true to your word, but commit to a standard you don't agree with and won't abide by." I could not win.

Another messenger of shame, according to VanVonderan, is coding. When love and acceptance are withheld from you if you dare to communicate a need straightforward, then you become good at skirting the issue in order to protect yourself. I might have a legitimate need for some help with a project, but when I ask for help, if I am accused of being selfish or stupid for having the need, or am accused of being incapable, you can bet I'm probably not going to ask for the help I need. I will find other ways to hint at my need, but I won't come out and admit to it.

My ex-husband and I tackled a huge project several years ago. We decided to build our own house. Literally. No kidding. It took us two years and plenty of blood, sweat and tears. Now, I would never have even entertained the thought were if not that he was incredibly capable, talented and a master at figuring stuff out. He wanted to give it a shot, and I followed his lead. There were several times when I felt incredibly inadequate.

I was his work crew and I was a woman. I was not much to bank on in the construction business, but I was always there at his side. We were both on a learning curve for most of the project, and it frustrated me that I didn't know everything I needed to know.

Rather than ask him how to do something, many times I would just get angry and start acting tough claiming that everything else was the problem. I didn't want to look stupid. I didn't want to let him down. I didn't want to disappoint. All I had to do was ask for help or be honest with what I was feeling. But I didn't feel safe. This was not because he would berate me for not knowing it all, but rather because I grew up in an environment where I was conditioned to believe that the direct approach was not always the safe approach.

Shame can also be communicated through a preoccupation with fault, blame and justice, according to VanVonderan. Someone has to pay!

Sometimes life is difficult. There is not always some specific person, situation or thing to pin stuff on. Sometimes stuff just happens. We live in a fallen world, and it is anything but perfect. In a shame-based system, someone has to be responsible. Someone is to blame, and that someone will be found at all costs!

I would often lay the blame on myself—just to make sure it's covered. I was not at all responsible for most of the things I would take responsibility for, but I would find a way to make it my fault. This is not healthy. I am much better than I used to be but sometimes this still rears its head.

There is a six-year gap between my older brother and myself and by the time I arrived on the scene, everyone was going in all different directions. I often felt as if I were an inconvenience.

In a shame-based system, children are often considered a nuisance, says VanVonderan. Children are messy, and noisy, and very seldom do they act like adults. They aren't supposed to, however, because children are children.

In my family, I often felt little tolerance for the fact that I was a child. Some of my most memorable spankings were from my father and they were because I was simply being childish. My running around and playing would easily irritate him. I remember getting into trouble on Saturday afternoon for eating an apple close enough for him to hear it. The sound annoyed him.

My sister tells a story about playing with my older brother upstairs in his room. Evidently they got a little rowdy and my father came bursting into the room with his belt flying. The pastor had dropped by for a visit, and my siblings' behavior in the room above was disruptive. Further, it must have tarnished the image my father wanted to project to the pastor that he was a good father and that he was in complete control of his children. What a message to send to a child. Your childish behavior made me look bad, so I will beat you and make you pay.

All of the forms in which shame can be communicated are not exclusive to this list. I am sure there are more. Perhaps these have led you to some memories of your own childhood where something was done or said to you that caused you to believe that you were a bad person and that you were not good enough. The messengers are different, but the messages they deliver have a deep and lasting impact.

THE IMPACT

VanVonderan warns that being surrounded by messages that communicate shame, whether they are blatant or subtle, will condition you. You do not live unaffected. The messages you receive become your truth. They shape how you relate to others and how you relate to yourself. They take root in the soil of your life and they put you into bondage with chains that grow heavier by the moment.

I grew up in a Christian home and I attended a Christian school from first grade through college. You would think that being surrounded by the church would have a positive impact on me. As I look back on my life, however, I can see the trail of my own brokenness, my bondage to chains I could not see and to lies that I believed to be true. I was a wounded soul trying with all my might to feel loved, accepted and not alone. These were, after all, needs I was created to have, weren't they?

The shaming messages I received along the way took root and I developed an identity that was based firmly in shame. I was convinced that there was something wrong with me. I believed that I was inadequate, that I was unlovable, that I was defective. Not only did I feel that within my family, my church, etc, but I also came to believe that even God was dissatisfied with me.

The church and Christian school environment in which I grew up was full of well-meaning people, but the focus seemed to be most prominently placed on how things looked. It felt like what man saw on the outward appearance was more important than the fact that God looked on the heart.

We had a strict dress code accompanied by a long list of do's and don'ts, and I came to believe that God somehow approved of me only if I wore dresses that fell below the knees and that did not have a slit in the side or back, and that did not have a zipper in the front like pants. God approved only of the Christian radio station that my church operated, and nothing else. God did not like it if I watched television at all, and going to movies caused even more points to be deducted from my score.

Anything closer than a 6" gap between a boy and me was absolutely unacceptable, and God only smiled on me if I attended church every time the doors were open, plus participated in Thursday night door-to-door visitation, or soul winning as some churches call it.

In my early years, it sounded like the Bible was manipulated to support every rule, even those that developed as a result of changing culture. It wasn't until I went to college that I learned that there was a distinction between a "biblical mandate" and an "institutional preference." Until then, every rule was the law as if God Himself had spoken it. I can live with an institution requiring that while you represent them as a student, you adhere to certain guidelines. What I had trouble with was the Bible being made to say whatever the institution wanted it to in order to mandate conduct and dress code.

I often felt as if I had no room to think for myself because everything was decided for me. I wasn't equipped with tools that taught how to come to good, healthy, righteous decisions on my own. Even my relationship with God was not truly my own, though I had been submerged in a Christian culture from the time I was born and had accepted Christ into my life when I was 13.

In school, we had devotions together as a class every morning, and chapel once a week. We were required to memorize passages of Scripture every month. I attended every Sunday School, every Sunday morning and evening service, Sunday night youth group, Wednesday night Prayer Meeting and all the other special revivals or missionary conference services that came up along the way. Still, God remained illusive. He was there with love and grace for me in some form initially to save me, but from then on out, it seemed as if it were up to me. I was lost in who I was told to be, and therefore, I lost who I was created to be.

It was easy for me to become detached from myself because I was in a system where I did not sense the safety and freedom to feel and think on my own. I had a disconnect between who I was and who I had to be in order to be accepted. I ended up being very detached from what I was feeling. Often, I just didn't know.

For me, my feelings often got garbled and skewed. No matter what I was feeling, it always seemed to come out as anger. There was no safety in my environment to feel what I was feeling. It wasn't ok just to be scared or overwhelmed. There was always the perceived danger that I would be cut down or my feelings would be dismissed. Even now, I sometimes react when my feelings are not validated. Sometimes I just want to know that it's ok to feel what I feel without judgment that I should or should not be feeling it.

Another struggle I have had is a tendency to base my sense of life, well-being, value and acceptance on anything and everything but God. This in its most basic and raw form is technically idolatry because it puts the power and focus on people and things other than God.

Often I have struggled with putting my value on what other people think or say about me. I have hungered for attention and wanted so much to be loved and accepted that I would try to find it where it wasn't meant to be found.

My church and school held an annual missions conference each fall. It would last for eight days, Sunday to Sunday, and several missionaries would come and participate. Just about every year, I would connect with one or two of those who attended, and would quickly become attached to them. Somehow, I felt valuable when I was around them. They liked me. They noticed me. They invested some time and attention in me. But, when the week was over, they would leave, and because they filled some deep-seated longing in me, I would be devastated.

Years back, I joined our church youth group to lead worship for their winter camp. It was held in the North Georgia Mountains at a YMCA campground. When I arrived, I was flooded with memories of my own camp experiences.

Many memories I had long since forgotten, but as I reflected I realized that my camp days were good days and that camp was a positive experience for me. It was a safe place for me to simply be me. The safety I felt there and the affirmation I received, however, was short lived. Camp only lasts a week.

After a week of having that need to be loved and accepted met by my camp counselors, the ride home and the nights to follow would often be full of tears. I would cry myself to sleep for days. I legitimately grieved.

The missionaries were only around for a short time. Camp only lasted a week. Basing value and self worth on things that are so uncertain, short-lived and prone to change is like building a house on sand. The foundation is shaky. It is uncertain. I couldn't count on it. How could I not be anxious? How could I not be exhausted? How could I not stay empty and wounded?

The way I viewed myself was definitely tweaked along the way, but the impact reached beyond that. Shaming messages not only affected how I related to myself, but it also had an impact on how I related to other people. I was hard on relationships ... very hard.

One of the areas VanVonderan mentions that is often affected by the web of shame is an unhealthy or non-existent set of personal boundaries. Boundaries are a good thing. They help govern your behavior toward others, and they help other people behave toward you.

Rivers have to have boundaries, or they would cause floods. A great example of this is the levees in New Orleans during Hurricane Katrina. They provided boundaries to keep the water out of the streets, but when the levees were breached, disaster came with the flood.

(For a more extensive look at healthy boundaries, check out "Boundaries" by Dr. Henry Cloud, Zondervan, 1992)

In a shame-based system where it is not ok to have a boundary and you are accused of being selfish if you say "no," that tends to make you hesitant to establish boundaries in the first place. Maybe you're afraid that if you decline that speaking engagement because your wife is sick and needs help caring for the children, you will look bad. You certainly don't want to look bad, or let anyone down, but sometimes saying no is the appropriate boundary to have.

When your identity is all wrapped up in how things look, and you are dependent on how things appear, then you tend to be extremely sensitive to everything that is going on around you. VanVonderan says that you tend to develop incredible radar so that you can get a jump on adjusting to whatever might be changing around you.

I have been known to have what some would call over-developed radar. As I said at the outset of this book, I have been a master editor. I can anticipate changes and interpret motives. At least I used to think that I could.

No one can judge the motives of another, and it only causes trouble when you think you can. Only God knows the true heart of a person. But so often we think we can play God and we react and adjust to what we think is going on. My sixth sense and my keen radar have actually been known to even create their own truth a time or two.

How ironic that as much as I dislike it when my motives are judged, somehow I thought it was ok to judge the motives of others. In a system based on shaming you for what is real, however, it's no wonder that all must stay built on what *appears* to be. It is shaky ground, but a place where I have lived. It is exhausting and is often a set up for a no-win situation.

Another consequence I have experienced because of the shaming messages I received, is that I have not had a good sense of what normal is. I became accustomed to abnormal behavior. Since it was normal for me, I mistook it to be normal for others as well.

Is it normal for a family to have meals together and not be allowed to talk to each other because dad is watching his favorite show on the TV across the room and doesn't want to be interrupted? Is it normal for inappropriate physical interactions to happen between siblings? Is it normal for a parent to force you into support system roles only because the other parent is too busy with his job to fill them? Is it normal for a teenager who chooses to stand on what she believes is right to be shamed and slandered for not conforming because it made her mother look bad? Maybe it is, maybe it isn't. Regardless, it certainly shouldn't be and it is far from healthy.

My father was a physician and sometimes, as all kids do, I would get hurt. Occasionally it was enough to warrant a trip down the street to his office so I could get some treatment.

When I was 3 or 4 years old, our neighbor's dog bit me on my forehead. I was terrified and I crying hysterically. I was legitimately traumatized by what had just happened to me, but the comfort I received that afternoon was not a loving, patient father reassuring me that I would be alright. There was no affirmation that it was understandable for me to be afraid, but rather, it was a gas mask applied to my mouth to render me unconscious so that I would shut up and let my dad take a look at the bite.

I remember that gas mask well. I saw it many times. I used to pull my little feet up to try and grab it away from my face. It came to the point where the mere threat of that mask would scare me still and quiet. This was normal to me. I didn't realize how disturbing this event was until I shared the story decades later with a dear friend of mine who sat in shock over the casualness of my perspective of this element of my childhood. This was not *normal*. This was cruel.

So many things become normal just because they are all you know. Sometimes it takes a backward glance from a new perspective in order to gain a more appropriate perspective that it truly was not normal at all. Much of what I experienced growing up was not normal, but it was what I knew. Only now as I look back can I see the dysfunction for what it was.

Another piece of my struggle with shame is that I have been wrought with the feeling that I don't belong. I mentioned that I am the youngest of six children and there is a six-year gap between my older brother and me.

Because of the age gap, there were many times when the older kids would be doing something special or going out somewhere. Either I could not be included because of my age or often they just did not want me to be included because I would spoil their fun. They used to speak in code around me so I wouldn't find out where they were going and beg to go with them.

Sometimes it felt as if I was an only child in a large family. I was insecure. I felt alone. I believed that I wasn't good enough to hang out with them, that I didn't qualify to really be a part of the family. I was a nuisance, or so I felt.

I spent much of my life not being comfortable in my own skin, feeling like I just didn't belong—no matter how much a part of things I actually was.

I have an African-American friend who has struggled with this sense of being alone in a crowd and feeling like she doesn't fit in. She is beautiful, she is smart and she is funny. She will brighten any room she walks into, but she has struggled with shame. We share a very similar story. She was telling me one day that she often, "feels her blackness when she's with white folks and doesn't feel black enough when she's with black folks." She struggles with feeling like she doesn't belong. This is a common thread for those bound by shame.

I based so much of my identity wrapped up in how things looked or on how well I behaved or performed. Because of this, my foundation couldn't be anything but shaky. Trust is hard to come by. Sometimes I still struggle with trust issues, even when it comes to trusting God.

I so desperately wanted to be loved unconditionally, to be accepted completely and to not be alone. All of these are basic needs. But people are not predictable, and you cannot control others. I have tried. Yes, often I have tried hard to manipulate and control those around me. I have tried to keep everything in my world as secure and predictable as I could possibly make it. But even so, underlying every relationship, there was always a lack of trust, and a deep-seated fear that I would be abandoned. I was convinced of it. I put so much focus on what others thought about me, but I could never rest because I was always certain that I would get hurt.

My mom was not always available to me because her hands were full with five other children. My father was not available to me because he was either at the office, or the hospital making rounds. When he was home, he wanted to be left alone.

In my most tender, formative years, I felt abandoned. My sister who sheltered me and cared for me moved out to go to college when I was 8, and with her leaving, it left room for others to introduce me to things about my body that an 8-year-old should never know. I began to put on a great deal of weight and I became very depressed. I was left feeling more alone than ever. As I grew, so did my defenses.

I became convinced that I would be hurt at some point, no matter how secure and healthy the relationship. I *knew* that eventually I would be abandoned. This is yet another common thread for those in the battle of shame, according to VanVonderan. Even after all of the healing that God has done in my life, sometimes it still pops up.

THE GRID

The battle with shame is real. The messages I received were real, whether intended or not. As a result, their impact is profound. When the shaming messages took root and I became convinced that there was something wrong with me, it affected every aspect of my life.

I developed defenses that may have been intended to protect me from more wounding, but they ended up reinforcing the shame I felt. It is a vicious cycle because no matter how much I wanted to be free, I was convinced that I was not worthy of freedom.

No matter what I heard or experienced, it is as if it got hung up in a grid. This grid intercepted everything that came in and twisted it to highlight the reality that I really didn't measure up after all.

Even if I received a message that was positive and intended to communicate love and acceptance, when it hit my grid, I was not able to receive it as positive and affirming. The grid twisted and deflected everything and it became my worst enemy.

VanVonderan talks about how some characteristics of the grid are unique to the individual who possesses it. It may take different forms or expressions based on the messages the individual has received over his or her lifetime.

Although everyone reacts to things differently, VanVonderan talks about some common components. Explaining the shame grid is difficult, and understanding it may be even more difficult, but you have to understand it in order to disarm it. Once it is in place, it is also very difficult to un-do.

I spent most of my life having no idea why different circumstances would push buttons and send me into a spiral. I didn't understand why I reacted to things the way I did or why I developed certain responses. As I got deeper into my healing, there were still times when the grid reared its head, but at least I came to know how to recognize it. As I have become more aware of my own grid, I have also become more aware of the grid when it presents itself in other people. It's enlightening.

Comedian Jeff Foxworthy is probably best recognized for his "You Might Be A Redneck" jokes. He provides us with a humorous list of qualifiers to help us identify whether or not we meet the criteria.

When I speak on shame and begin to share the components of the shame grid, I am often reminded of the phrase "You might be a redneck"; only my lists all end with "You might be shame-based." Truth is, if you identify some of these things in your life, you might be struggling with a bit of a shame grid.

Most of the main bullet points about the shame grid are once again pulled from Jeff VanVonderan's book, but they are woven into my story. Perhaps this chapter will help you identify and consequently dismantle your own grid, as well as help you relate in a more healthy manner to those around you. You may find it very enlightening. It was for me.

One of the first indicators that you might have a shame grid in place is if you tend to say things to yourself such as, "You are such an idiot", "You can't do anything right", "You are so stupid!" The grid turns you into your own prosecuting attorney. You put yourself on the stand and throw accusations and blame at yourself. You berate yourself but all that this does is reinforce the shame and defectiveness you already feel. It is the grid in action and it keeps you enslaved to the shaming messages that you have bought and believed to be true.

I was in an up-scale restaurant a few years ago to purchase two gift certificates. I was going to purchase one on a personal credit card, and the other on my business credit card. The gift certificates were to be in two different amounts, and the hostess ended up putting the wrong amount on the wrong card. The transaction was confusing, and she made a mistake. What struck me is that she kept calling herself "stupid" and "idiot." I recognized the grid right away and I felt compelled to tell her kindly that she was not stupid, but that she had made a mistake, and that there is a big difference between the two. I felt compassion for her because I could see that she was in bondage to shaming messages because her grid told me so. I spoke some truth to her that day, and I pray that it made a difference.

Mistakes. No one likes to make mistakes. When you have received the message that you have to be perfect in order to be loved and accepted, mistakes simply are not tolerated. They document imperfection. If you overreact to making mistakes, you may have a shame grid in place.

I hate making mistakes, but it happens. No one is perfect. It is interesting to me that I have much more grace for the mistakes of others than I have grace for my own. I have gotten better at this as I continue on my journey, but I do still tend to react to my mistakes.

I have also had the tendency to react to situations where I perceive that I made a mistake, when actually there was no mistake at all. Our church held a children's musical one Christmas and we needed to use one of the exterior doors as an entrance for one of the characters during the performance. I was asked to make a sign for the door indicating that it was not an entrance, and was given direction on how the sign should read. I made the sign as instructed, and placed it where asked, but when the person who wanted the sign put up saw it, she realized that it might be confusing the way it read. I immediately got defensive and reacted as if I had made a mistake, even though I had not. The situation had gotten skewed as it passed through my grid. There was no mistake. I had done what I had been asked to do. All that I needed to do was make a small adjustment on the original design so as to make the sign more effective. I had not failed. I had not made a mistake, but my grid got in the way and it caused me to react.

Another indicator that you may be struggling with shame, according to VanVonderan, is that you tend to feel over-responsible and find a way to blame everything on yourself even if you had nothing to do with it.

I was walking into a friend's house one afternoon and Dr. Phil was on TV. At the moment I came into earshot, I heard him say to a couple on the show that, "You can't hold yourself responsible for things you can't control". This statement struck me as a profound truth, yet somehow this truth had eluded me. This has been a big issue for me over the years. There were times when my ex-husband was working on a project around the house, and things were not going well. Even if I was not involved in any way, I somehow felt as if I needed to apologize for the frustration he was feeling.

I remember one situation that occurred after I began to realize that I was not an all-powerful being with control over everything and everyone. He was very frustrated and angry because a job he was doing around the house had turned into an all out battle. Historically, this situation was known to turn into an argument between us because I would somehow feel like his frustration was my fault. Since I never wanted to fail, I would get angry with myself, which in turned expressed itself in lashing out at him, thus fueling his frustration and anger. The cycle would continue.

On this particular day, I realized that I was not responsible for the way the job was going. I had done nothing wrong and it was not my fault. I was only there trying to help him. In realizing this, I was able to encourage and affirm him. By not playing my role in the cycle or playing the victim, I was able to help diffuse it. I didn't take it personally, but rather, was able to love him through it. It made all the difference in the world.

If you have difficulty in allowing yourself to feel and express legitimate needs, you may be struggling with shame. The grid tells you that having a need is equal to being selfish, or worse yet, inadequate, so you end up refusing to allow valid needs to be met.

Going back to the example of when we built our house, there were countless times when I didn't have a clue what I was doing, or how to do it. I was so far out of my comfort zone on so many occasions. I needed information, I needed help carrying things and I needed help holding things in place. Each of these is a genuine need, but there were times when I thought I would look bad or stupid if I asked for help, so I'd fight my way through it on my own.

Often I would choose to risk hurting myself by trying to move or carry something way too heavy for me to move, rather than to appear weak. I didn't feel like my need was enough to bother him over—even though he was always always there available and wanting to help me. The grid frequently would not let me ask for help and it put me in a position where I was set up to fail. Again, this reinforced the shame I felt.

I mentioned earlier about having well-developed radar, but with a shame grid in place, you can't trust it. That keen sense of awareness you have of all that is going on around you makes you notice things and adjust to them, but if you notice something is wrong and you point it out, then somehow you have become the problem. This goes back to the "Can't Talk" rule mentioned earlier. The grid tells you that you are really the one with the problem, or it tells you that whatever it is you noticed isn't really that bad. You have great radar, but you don't trust it.

In a shame-based system, it is not OK to have needs, to notice things, or to break those unwritten rules. Consequently, says VanVonderan, the grid also makes you good at coding. You wouldn't dare speak straight because it isn't safe to do so in a shaming environment. If you tend to speak around the issue rather than speaking directly because you are afraid to, you may be in the struggle of shame.

One thing that plagued me for most of my life was that I had an extremely difficult time playing, or having guilt—free fun. Some of my most memorable spankings were directly connected to my acting like a child when it should have been expected of me to be childish. It was difficult for me to cut loose and be carefree. I was way too cautious, too precise, and too serious. I was never the kid to get involved with pranks at camp, or to enjoy "April Fools" jokes. I never really enjoyed being silly or looking foolish.

God has did a work on me in this area by giving me two precious friends who were quite good at being silly and having fun. I often joke that when the three of us were together, it was my job to keep them out of jail! They came

35

up with some crazy idea and I would just sit back and shake my head.

[Note: Life is way too short to be so serious all the time, as we are too often reminded. One of those precious friends died of cancer in December 2007. Her life and legacy live on, however, and I am thankful for the fingerprints she left on my life.]

When you come from a system of shaming messages that tells you that you are not good enough, your self-image is very negative and you develop the expectation that you will be abandoned, hurt or let down. Because of this, you may in turn have difficulty receiving what you need or want. You may want or need something very legitimately, but believing that you do not deserve it, you push it away. If you play the 'come here, go away' game, you may be experiencing yet another part of the shame grid.

This is one area that I had personally mastered along the way. No matter how much I needed or wanted something, I could not allow myself to receive it. I believed that I was not worthy of it and that I did not deserve it, or I presumed that it would disappear once I got it, so I pushed it away. This has plagued many relationships in my life. I have had a difficult time relaxing into friendships and trusting them, no matter how solid.

Along with the 'come here, go away' game, there were times when I would actually try to sabotage friendships because I was convinced that the person would leave me eventually anyway. I thought that I may as well get it over with. When you have a shame grid in place, the love, acceptance and value that you need and want cannot be received because it collides with that deep-seated sense of shame and the belief that you don't deserve it, or that you are not good enough.

This issue also made me very possessive and jealous in my friendships. I was finding my value in my friends and in what other people thought about me. I was banking on their acceptance and my value depended on them. I held on for dear life, yet at the same time, I couldn't allow myself to rest in it and receive it because I felt unworthy of it. I did everything I could to get people to like me, but when they did, I pushed them away. It was exhausting.

Another indicator of a shame-based identity, according to VanVonderan, is if you have a hard time receiving gifts. Again, it collides against the grid that says you don't deserve it. This was an extremely difficult area for me throughout my lifetime. Birthdays and Christmases were horrible for me in years past because receiving a gift when you don't feel you deserve it does not sit well when a shame grid is in place.

One Christmas, my ex-husband wanted to surprise me with what he thought was an amazing gift, but when I opened it, I could not allow myself to receive it as a token of his love for me, and his desire for me to have it. It smashed against my shame grid. It conflicted with my practical, serious side that said we couldn't afford it and that I didn't need it. Obviously, it robbed him of the joy of giving me the gift, and it robbed me of the joy of receiving it. My reactions to his attempts at surprising me or giving me special gifts caused him to be fearful to do anything at all for me. I was faced with having to carefully undo a situation that I had caused by not allowing him to give to me freely. He was understandably afraid because of the way I had reacted in the past.

Whether in relationships or in the workplace, or even with a personal goal as basic as losing weight, any success in general fights against the grid. It collides with that view of yourself that you are not worth it. The grid will make you want to sabotage successes and will also hold you back with fear that if you start something, you might fail. People wounded by shaming messages end up being very good at procrastinating!

When your value is based on uncertain externals, and you are preoccupied with the way things look, the status of your environment and the behavior of people, you end up expending a great deal of energy trying to control all of those factors. If you tend to be over-controlling, you may be struggling with shame.

The grid causes you to want to fix, improve or adjust anything that might threaten your sense of worth. It also causes you to try and punish anyone who does not act the way you need or want them to act. People struggling with shame issues tend to be over-controlling in order to try and make everything in their lives just so. This is a pointless battle, however, because things are never just so, and as hard as you try, you cannot control other people.

In my own life, I was extremely hard on relationships because of this area in particular. Any component of the shame grid tends to be hard on relationships, but this one has wounded many people in my life.

I have a very precious friend whom I love dearly. In the early years of our friendship, she was meeting my deep-rooted need to be loved and accepted. She loved me and communicated value to me. The fact that she was communicating this affirmation to me is not a bad thing in itself. What was bad is that I was banking on it to make me feel valuable and worthy. She was my source of affirmation and because I was relying on her so much, I tried to control her. I didn't want anything to change. I would feel threatened whenever she would talk about other friends, or when new friends would come into her life. I was unable to be happy when opportunities came up for her that did not include me. I would in a very real sense, punish her if she did anything that introduced a perceived threat.

It is hard for me to admit that, but it took time for me to see what I was doing. It was unfair, unkind and in some cases, downright cruel. I hurt her many times along the way because of my own insecurities. I lived in this underlying fear that I would lose her, yet I would run from her or push her away.

God, in His great mercy and grace, gave my friend eyes to see beyond my behavior and into my potential. He used her greatly to help facilitate the healing and growth behind the writing of this book. I am forever grateful that she chose to stick it out with me.

THE CYCLE

I don't believe anyone sets out to intentionally shame another. What I do believe is that if you have no healthy behavior by which to measure your behavior, then you will continue the unhealthy patterns. It becomes your normal. Many people who are parents today grew up with parents who communicated these messages to them. They did not have good parenting skills modeled to them, and consequently, they may not know how to parent their children any differently. It is a cycle. People that are wounded tend to wound others.

My parents both grew up in homes that were full of shaming messages. It is within great probability that my grandparents grew up in a similar environment. I can say that with some confidence because we learn what we see. We imitate what we know.

I was born later in my parents' lives, so my grandparents were much older when I arrived. I have some memories of them, but not many as they all passed away while I was still young. But I do remember my maternal grandparents who lived just a few doors down from where I grew up. Aside from the memory of going over there on Saturday nights to watch "The Lawrence Welk Show" (yes, I am that old!) and eat pink wintergreen candies, I remember the two of them bickering back and forth quite a bit. I didn't know much of what was going on, but I could feel the tension even in my young years.

I didn't have any perspective on shame issues when I was younger, but I do know that my dad's life has shown evidence of much brokenness. I am confident that I can connect it back to the generation before him, and probably the generation before that. It is a cycle. We imitate what we see; we operate from what we have learned.

If you see someone caught in the snare of shame, you can rest assured they were not born that way. Babies arrive with no baggage. Their slates are a pure and clean as a fresh snowfall. But once they are here, they learn from their environment, they learn from the systems of which they are a part.

My paternal grandparents were both pretty strong people. My grandmother in particular was a very hard, controlling woman from what little I saw and from what my older siblings have told me. Somewhere along the way, it seems as if my dad missed the affirmation, acceptance and love he needed when he was growing up. Consequently, he is a very insecure man.

He has always been a prominent member of our small town because he was "the" local doctor. He did everything from delivering babies to caring for the elderly, back in the day. He has literally saved dozens, if not hundreds of lives. But somewhere along the way, he developed a sense that he was not good enough and that he did not measure up. He has spent a great deal of energy over his 80+ years trying to prove over and over again that he is worthy and valuable.

There were several times over my life when my dad would say to me, "Tell them who your daddy is," as if that could fix anything. Even in my adult life, he would find occasion to say this to me. I never could figure out how this might help, but somehow, saying this to me made him feel important.

My mother is a perfectionist, and is always concerned with what other people think about her. When in good conscience I could not sign that behavior and conduct contract in order to be on the singing team in high school, my mother caught a great deal of fallout from my decision.

She volunteered as the school nurse and attended the weekly staff meetings. During one meeting shortly after the contract episode, the pastor of the church and school spoke in judgment about the parents who could not control their children and force them to sign it. My decision to be honest made my mother feel as if she were a bad parent, which in turn caused her to try and make me feel badly. Because of my mother's own shame grid this particular issue put a significant rift in our relationship. This lasted for a couple of years.

I was talking to my sister recently about how things were in my family before I arrived on the scene and it was enlightening. My whole life has been spent in the church, but I never knew where that started. I found out that after my parents moved back to my mom's hometown after my dad graduated from medical school, they began to attend the little Baptist church just down the road. A new pastor came in and wanted the church to disconnect from the Baptist Association with which they were affiliated because it was "too liberal". This caused the church to split, and my parents went with this pastor to start a new church in a neighboring town.

According to my sister, this is where religion came into the family. She said that we children were my parent's showpieces, and we were all made to look and behave in such a way as to make them look like good parents. Our behavior as children directly impacted how my parents felt about themselves. They were finding their value in our behavior. The problem with this is that children are not predictable. Sometimes they are messy. The foundation my parents were standing on in order to find their value and worth was shaky.

As my eyes have become more open to patterns of shame, I have become more aware of those patterns in others. I never knew anything different than the way things were, but as I look back on my family, church and school environments, I can see the shame at work.

Both of my parents are in their 80's and are only recently beginning to fail in health. I love them dearly and am thankful for the positive influences they have had on me. They provided well for me and made sure I got a good college education. They have supported and encouraged me along the way and I am thankful for them.

As the roles are reversing between us in their sunset years, they have a huge respect for me and for the woman I have become. Although they did the best they could in raising us with the tools they had been given, I know they live with many regrets. Their shame grids have convinced them that they were failures as parents.

I am sad for them. I am sad that their lives have been so difficult and so unfulfilling even through their successes. I am sad that they have been bound by the shaming messages they received from the generation before them. I am sad that each of my siblings now struggles with shame issues in some form or another. We have all had to fight our way through spiritual and emotional healing because the cycle has been passed down. I am sad that as my parents come to the end of their lives, they are still fighting for some sense of being ok.

All of us learn from our parents, and unfortunately, many of us have learned bad habits in relating to each other. Many of us have received shaming messages that have impacted us deeply, and chances are, we have passed those messages along to others around us or those behind us.

Thankfully, the cycle does not have to continue. The shame cycle can stop with you. It can stop with me. We do not have to continue to live in the "normal" we have known up until now. Freedom is available. Healing is within reach. We can live in truth, rather than in deception. We can re-define "normal".

Shame is a deep-seated issue. I mentioned earlier the difference between shame and guilt. Guilt is behavior—based. You can change the feeling of guilt by changing the behavior. Guilt is related to *doing* wrong, but shame is connected to a sense of *being* wrong. Shame is your belief that there is something wrong with you and that you don't measure up, that you are not loved, valued and accepted unconditionally.

Unfortunately, for those that struggle with shame, new behaviors are the focus of the solution. If only you do this, or don't do that, or if you look this way or that way. Perhaps you should attend church more. Maybe you should visit the sick or feed the poor. Maybe you should pray more, attend recovery meetings, tithe, etc. Whatever the behavior might be, it will never work. Changing your behavior will never change how you view yourself.

You cannot perform your way out of shame because performance does not cause shame. Shame causes you to strive to behave and perform but striving only makes you tired.

One spring, my ex-husband decided to plant a garden in the lower area of our yard. He spent several hours tilling up the soil and planting rows of various fruits and vegetables, carefully marking each row and watering the area. Over time, nothing but weeds came up. We had little hints of plants trying their best, and an odd, pitiful squash or two, but nothing ever grew. There was no harvest.

The next year, the same thing happened. The seeds he planted were fine. The area had sunlight most of the day. He made sure it got plenty of water. He was doing all the right things, but still, nothing would grow.

We were in Georgia and Georgia dirt is very acidic. It is red, not brown, and evidently, it is not garden-friendly. Even after treating the area with lime to try to neutralize the acid, we still barely had a garden, and what we did have was pathetic.

Not wanting to give up, the following year, my husband went to a nearby farm and got a truckload of manure to spread out and mix in with the dirt. He specifically focused on the soil trying to create conditions that would be favorable for growing a garden. The problem was not in all that was happening above the surface, our garden woes continued to be in the dirt. We never did figure out the correct combination required to make the ground fertile. The problem is in the soil. No matter what you do above ground, no matter how neatly you plant the rows, no matter how much you water it, if the soil is bad, you will have a bad crop … or you will have no crop at all.

So often we focus on the externals. Many counselors offer people more things to do. Even the church has been known to offer solutions that involve doing more. But behaviors and performance will only make you tired. If you want to attack the shame issue, VanVonderan stresses, you have to deal with the soil.

"National Lampoon's Christmas Vacation" is one of my all-time favorite movies. I watch it every year. There is one scene where the family is gathered around the table for a 'big, old fashioned, family Christmas' dinner with the grandparents, aunts and uncles, and cousin Eddie and his family.

Clark Griswold, the man of the house, is just about to carve the gorgeous turkey made by Eddie's wife. It looks pristine, straight out of the oven, golden brown. It looks mouth-watering beautiful ... until Clark starts to cut into it. With one poke of the fork, the turkey cracks wide open. It is brittle, dry and empty inside—it is a complete disaster.

How often do we spend our lives looking good on the outside, but we are completely dry, brittle and empty on the inside? We spend so much energy on the way we look or perform, but inside, we are dead. We are in essence 'dead men walking'. This is not God's desire for us. The Bible says, "It is for freedom that Christ has set us free", Galatians 5:1. God does not want us to be enslaved to the shaming messages we received. He wants us to walk in freedom. He wants us to be fulfilled and happy. His desire for us is that we live consistently with who we are in Him. God wants our insides to line up with our outsides.

I was born straight into the church nursery and have gone to church my entire life since then. I attended a Christian school where every morning we would have devotions together as a class. I was required to memorize a different passage of Scripture every month of every school year for 12 years. We had chapel services once a week. The entire curriculum was Bible-based. It was expected that I attend church every time the doors were open.

I went from the Christian school to attend a Christian college where we had daily chapel services. I have a minor in Bible. You could say that I know a thing or two about God. I actually know quite a bit, but knowing about God means little or nothing if you do not truly *know* God.

Coming from a shame-based system, it is as if the shaming messages form a barrier between your brain and your heart. If all of what you know in your head stays in your head and never settles into your heart, you will never know the freedom that God has intended.

In his book, "Tired of Trying to Measure Up," Jeff VanVonderan says that, "the Christian life is a process of learning to live consistently with who we already are in Christ." God wants us to KNOW Him, not just know about Him.

When you get ready to go on vacation, you probably look at brochures, or search your desired location on the Internet that provides you with a virtual tour of your hotel or potential vacation experience so you can make the best decisions. No matter how much research you do, no matter how many pictures you see or how much you read about it, you never really know your destination until you have actually been there.

I had the privilege of traveling quite a bit when growing up because my dad would lead tour groups consisting mostly of his elderly patients to Hawaii. He would go just about every other year and it was a perk for me to go with them the most times because I was the youngest.

I absolutely love Hawaii! I know the feeling of waking up the morning after the 9-hour flight and seeing the sunrise over Diamond Head on Oahu. I know the smell of the full breakfast buffet at Duke's Canoe Club, eating on the lanai overlooking Waikiki Beach and sharing crumbs with the Aloha Birds. I have watched the sunrise over Haleakala Crater and have strolled Front Street in Lahaina, Maui. I have walked on old lava flow fields on the Big Island of Hawaii and seen steam rise from the vents on an active volcano. I know which sailing charters to take and which luaus to attend. I have not just read about Hawaii. I have been there.

As His children, God does not want us to be satisfied with merely reading the brochure or filling our heads with knowledge about the journey; He wants us to actually take the journey.

THE PROCESS

The problem of shame runs deep. You cannot perform your way out of it. You can't undo its damage by changing how you act. You have to deal with it at the most basic level. You need a radical transformation of your inner self. You need a conversion—not a conversion experience like when you first accepted the gift of salvation through the blood of Jesus and made the journey from death to eternal life, but a "second conversion"—one that kicks your relationship with God to a deeper level. We all need a conversion that moves us from knowing God as the One who saved us, to truly understanding that God is crazy in love with us. We need to be transformed.

In Romans 12:2, Paul writes, *"Do not conform any longer to the pattern of this world, but be transformed by the renewing of your mind"*. The word used for "transformed" in the Greek is "metamorphoo" which means to change from the inside out. This is where we get our word for "metamorphosis." (http://www.preceptaustin.org/romans_122.htm)

God is so gracious to provide us with practical illustrations in the natural realm to help us understand things in the spiritual realm. He shows us in Matthew 6 that we do not need to fret about our needs being met because of how he takes care of the flowers and the birds. He points out in Matthew 7 and Luke 11 that an earthly father desires to give good gifts to his children and compares that to how much more He wants to give us good gifts. The example in the natural helps us get a handle on a spiritual truth that might otherwise not sink in.

One profound example of this is the process of metamorphosis. Metamorphosis is fascinating and it takes place all around us every day.

The official definition from www.wikipedia.com is that **Metamorphosis** is *"a biological process by which an animal physically develops after birth or hatching, involving a conspicuous and relatively abrupt change in the animal's form or structure through cell growth and differentiation."*

An obvious example would be the monarch butterfly. It begins as a caterpillar, gets into a cocoon, and 2-6 weeks later, it emerges as a beautiful butterfly.

There are two types of metamorphosis, one is "incomplete", the other "complete". Incomplete metamorphosis is where the adult has some resemblance to the infant stage. Some examples of insects that undergo an incomplete metamorphosis are cockroaches, praying mantises, dragonflies and grasshoppers.

Opposite of incomplete metamorphosis is complete metamorphosis, in which the adult has absolutely no resemblance at all to the infant stage. This is what happens to the monarch butterfly. It appears with no hint of what it started out as. (http://en.wikipedia.org/wiki/Metamorphosis)

This is the business God is in when it comes to our lives. He wants to transform us completely into His image, with no hint of what we were before. For the monarch, metamorphosis is the transformation from crawling to flying. The same can be said for us!

One of the most beautiful aspects of the word '*metamorphoo*' is that this Greek word is in the passive tense. Reaching back to your English grammar days in school, you may remember that there are two tenses for verbs. Verbs can be active, or verbs can be passive.

Verbs in the active tense show the subject acting: "Tommy hit the ball". But verbs in the passive tense show something else acting on the subject: "The ball was hit by Tommy". '*Metamorphoo*' is in the passive voice, meaning that the process of "being transformed" is actually something done *to* us, not something done *by* us. Our transformation is not something we do; it is done to us as a result of the renewing of our minds, according to Romans 12:2.

Often we put so much energy into trying to fix our environment, our circumstances or ourselves. We waste time and effort striving for love, acceptance and value, all of which are legitimate needs, but we try to meet them in illegitimate and inappropriate ways. The struggle of shame becomes a struggle to survive. There is no rest. There is no reprieve. There is no peace. It is exhausting.

I came to a point years ago where my struggle was so strong that I literally hated being me. All that I desired but could not receive tormented me. I was constantly in turmoil and exhausted by my fight. It took too much energy to be me and I was dying inside. What I did not realize was that I was fighting for what was already mine. Like a dog chasing his tail, I was expending all of my energy on what I already had, I just didn't know it.

THE FIGHT

In the struggle with shame issues, if we are going to fight at all, we need to be sure we are fighting the right fight. Rather than beating against the air and wasting energy, why not fight a battle that we can win?

We get the word "fight" from the Greek word "agon", which means to do combat or to strive earnestly. It is the word from which we get the English word 'agony'. (http://www.antioch. com.sg/cgi-bin/bible/vines/get_defn.pl?num=1041#A1)

Battles are not easy. Battles are not pleasant. Battles are bloody and hard. Battles are agonizing. If there is to be a battle at all, make sure you are fighting the right one. Fighting behaviors and circumstances will never work. It will only make you tired.

In my journey, I have found two fights worth fighting. The first is the fight to rest. This is a foreign concept to those in the struggle of shame. Rest has never been an option. It has always been about performance, never about resting. We need to fight to rest from our efforts to gain love, acceptance and value from people and things, and instead, fight to rest in the love, acceptance and value that we already have in God. He has decided our value by what He has done. We need to rest in His performance.

A few years ago, my friend's son was given an old rusty, beat up Oldsmobile Cutlass. This car was in bad shape. It had lived its entire life in the Chicago area and had all of the rust damage you would expect from a car living in snow country.

He drove it for a short while until some road debris smashed the windshield. It then sat covered in the driveway until all the tires went flat. It got to the point where he realized that he would never personally restore it and that it was nothing more than an eyesore, so he decided to put it on eBay and see what happened.

To everyone's amazement, the car sold within a few hours to a couple that lived three states away. They drove through the night with a trailer and cash in hand, picked it up and drove it back home. I would not have paid anything for that rust bucket. But to them, the car had value. They saw its potential. It was what they were looking for. That car had no value in and of itself. Its value was determined by what the buyers were willing to pay for it.

The same is true of us. Our value is not dependent on us; God has already determined our value by the price He was willing to pay. God decided that we were worth the death of

His Son, Jesus and has offered us value and acceptance at His own expense. We are accepted. We are loved unconditionally. We are valued. We are not alone. God has already purchased our acceptance with the blood of His Son. We did not earn it; it has always been ours and we can rest in what He has done. What's even better is that it is impossible to lose what we did not earn. It has always been, and always will be. We have to fight to rest in this truth.

In the process of metamorphosis, after the caterpillar gets into that cocoon, it must come to a place of complete stillness and rest. It must cease all activity in order for the transformation to begin to occur. Fight to rest. Stop striving to perform.

I am reminded of the song *"I Still Haven't Found What I'm Looking For"* by the rock group, U2. How often we keep fighting and never find what we're looking for. The truth is, however, we actually already have what we're looking for. We don't have to look for it; we just have to rest in it.

God is at work in each of us and He will complete what He has started. He is the One who is ultimately responsible for our growth, not us. The Bible is pretty clear on this: I Corinthians 3:7, *"Neither he who plants, nor he who waters is anything, but only God who makes things grow"*. Philippians 1:6, *"Being confident of this, that he who began a good work in you will carry it on to completion until the day of Christ Jesus"*. And Philippians 2:13, *"for it is God who works in you to will and to act according to His good purpose."* Transformation is not our job. Relax and allow God to do what He's doing. You can count on Him to complete it.

The secret is making a choice to yield to God's activity in

our lives. So often we keep trying to drive. The bumper stickers that read, "God is my co-pilot" are actually quite sad, not to mention scary. If God is your *co-pilot*, you are in big trouble. God should be in the pilot's seat—always!

One Sunday a few years back, I gave the announcements during our church service. It wasn't anything fancy; it was just a few announcements. At the time, however, I was in the middle of a great deal of turmoil over my role and my calling in ministry. There was a season where I was angry with God because He wasn't doing things the way I thought they should be done. I was jealous of His calling on other people and at the same time, denying the uniqueness of my own.

It was an extremely frustrating season for me. I would fight for what I wasn't supposed to have, yet fight to deny what was mine to claim. It seems so foolish now as I look back, but at the time it was a very real battle and a major waste of energy.

After church that particular Sunday, a dear friend of mine came to me and sweetly put her hands on my face and told me that I was so gifted, and that God's anointing was all over me. I thought this was so strange because I had only given the announcements. How can that be anointed? But my friend saw something very significant and powerful in me that morning. She told me that the call of God was all over my life, and that no matter how much I fought it, it was still God's call and it was only His to give, remove or change.

There is nothing I could do to get rid of God's call on me. It is simply there. This was a profound statement to me for I had never considered the frailty of my denial of God's call on my life. How arrogant of me to think I had control over God!

57

She then said something that was extremely poignant and has become a marker moment for me. She said that I needed only to walk in what God had called me to do, and that as I chose to step out in obedience and yield to that plan, the stuff I had been continuing to struggle with would start to break away.

Those words had a significant impact on me, and from where I stand now, I can see clearly that what she said would be true is exactly what happened. As I began to get comfortable in my own skin and be who God had created me to be, and do what was uniquely mine to do, I began to find more and more freedom from the chains I had worn over the years.

God was at work then and He is continuing to fulfill His purposes in my life today. It is so much easier to lean into Him and yield to the process rather than fight and struggle in a battle I can never win. The caterpillar must give in completely to the process of metamorphosis, and in the same way, we must give in completely to the work that God wants to accomplish in us. Rest. Relax.

We also need to rest physically. There is something to be said about resting in God's presence and finding moments of stillness. Life is busy and schedules are packed. There is always something or someone clamoring for our time and attention, but the process of transformation requires rest. There is immense value in simply being with God as His child and resting in His presence.

Author and speaker, Brennan Manning has said that the secret is to *"spend times of stillness with God. Communing with Abba in the innermost places of your soul will transform your perspective of reality. It will enable you to recognize God's love and care in the middle of the chaos of life."* He says *"our longing to know who we really are will never be satisfied until we embrace solitude (not loneliness) but genuine solitude where we discover that we are totally loved by God."* (Posers, Fakers and Wannabes, NavPress, Colorado Springs, 2003)

No matter how busy we are in life, we still tend to find time for the things that are important to us. We all have the ability to cram things into a schedule that has no openings if that particular thing is something we place value on. We always make time for our priorities. Why then do we often have trouble finding time to spend with God? Why do we have such a hard time making God a priority?

For those of us who have struggled with shame, we have become so conditioned to **do**. Everything has depended upon appearances or performing. But you can sit still. You can rest. God has already sealed your value. Rest. Listen.

Wait. Often God will speak in silence if you are still before Him and know that He is God (Psalm 46:10). Don't let the noise of the stuff of life drown out the still, small voice of the Father who loves you beyond measure. *"Make every effort to enter into that rest"* (Hebrews 4:10). We need to fight to rest.

The second fight worth fighting is the fight for faith. According to thefreedictionary.com, faith is "a confident belief in the truth, value or trustworthiness of a person, idea or thing. It is a belief that does not rest on logical proof or material evidence." (http://www.thefreedictionary.com/faith)

The Bible talks about faith as being "sure of what we hope for and certain of what we do not see" (Hebrews 11:1). This evidently was not meant to come easy or Paul would not have encouraged us in I Timothy 6:12 to *"Fight the good fight of faith"*. We have to fight for it.

It is one thing to rest in what God has already done for us, but we also need to fight to believe that what He says is true. We need to trust that our value and acceptance is already ours, and it has always been.

I have spent a great deal of my life immersed in Christianity. I have plenty of head knowledge, but all of what you know about God will never settle into your heart until you have the faith to believe that it is true. Do you really trust God? Do you really believe that He is crazy about you? It is through this fight of faith that we come to know and rest in what has always been there. Brennan Manning says, *"Faith is the courage to accept our acceptedness."* (Posers, Fakers and Wannabes, NavPress, Colorado Springs, 2003)

In his book, "Velvet Elvis," Rob Bell, author and pastor of Mars Hill in Grand Rapids, Michigan, talks about a time when he and his father were in a restaurant eating a meal. When it came time to pay the bill, their server told them that another patron in the store had already taken care of it. He recalls that at that time, he was forced to make a decision on whether or not to act in the reality that the bill had been paid, or to deny it and try to pay it again. He told this story to make the point that every day, we choose the reality in which we will operate.

Will we choose to believe that the blood of Jesus has already paid our bill, or will we choose to perform and behave with a wasted effort to try and pay our own? Will we choose to believe that all of what God says about us is true, or will we allow all of our head knowledge to stay in our heads? Will we choose to live our lives as if we owe nothing and that all of the love, acceptance and value we have so desperately craved has been ours all along, or will we exhaust ourselves trying to earn what we already have? The choice is ours.

God has already paid our bill. There are no hoops to jump through. There is no behavior contract to sign. God is not a cop waiting around the corner looking for a reason to bust us, nor is He sitting in the dark at the back of the theatre as a talent show judge scoring our every move. He can love you no more than He does right now, and He can love you no less.

We were created to walk in freedom. *"It is for freedom that Christ has set us free, be not entangled again with the yolk of slavery"*, Galatians 5:1. I love how that verse reads in The Message version by Eugene Peterson. It says *"Christ has set us free to live a free life. So take your stand! Never again let anyone put a harness of slavery on you."* Take your stand, my friends! Fight to rest in what God has already done and in what you already have in Him, and fight for the faith to believe that all of it is true.

THE TRUTH

My fight and struggle for love, acceptance and value hung heavily on me like iron chains for most of my life. The weight of it was unbearable. I hated being in my skin. I felt empty and worthless. No matter how hard I tried, I believed I could never measure up. I was convinced of my defectiveness and any joy I might catch the scent of was quickly blown away by my inability to receive it. It was as if I was cursed with an unquenchable thirst, with a cup of cool water just outside my reach and no matter how hard I tried, I could never reach it. My striving to do so only made my chains grow tighter. My relationships were suffering. My job was suffering. My marriage was suffering. I was desperate and I was exhausted.

I live near a Civil War battlefield in Georgia called Kennesaw Mountain. If you have ever seen "real" mountains, you would most likely laugh at the term "mountain" being assigned to these two bumps that raise up all by themselves in the middle of an otherwise relatively flat terrain in the northwest suburbs of Atlanta. But it served its purpose during the war and allowed the soldiers to get to higher ground. Kennesaw Mountain was the south's last stand before General Sherman stormed into Atlanta in 1864.

Today, the mountain serves as a popular recreational park with a Civil War museum as well as large groomed lawns for kite flying, picnicking or playing Frisbee. The park is also a popular spot for hikers as it provides numerous trails with varying degrees of difficulty on and around the mountain.

There was a season in which I was hiking pretty regularly for exercise. Often I would walk with a friend, but there were times when I walked alone. Many people hike Kennesaw Mountain every day, so I was never completely alone, but there were days when I was left to my own thoughts rather than engaged in breathless conversation as I pushed myself up the trail.

One day my struggle with myself was so consuming that I began to fear for my well-being. I needed help. I needed to be rescued. I was in self-destruct mode, and I knew it. Something had to break, or I would break. So I went for a hike. I took the hardest trail because I wanted to sweat. Like Jacob in the Old Testament, I wanted to fight this thing out. I was desperate. I was desperate to hear God.

I cried out to God asking Him to speak to me. I wanted to hear Him. I needed to know He was there. I needed to know that He noticed me. With every step, with every breath, with every heartbeat, I was laying myself out there. "God, You have to do something! I need You! Talk to me!"

And with a sweet stillness and calm, I heard Him gently say, "What would you like to talk about?"

It stunned me at first. Did I really just hear that? It was so real that I swear God was walking right beside me. He was as real as the rocks beneath my feet. My pace relaxed and I started to breathe more slowly, and we talked. God had heard my cry for help. He had met me in my struggle, and with just a word, He began to break the bondage away from me that afternoon, and lead me further into the freedom He had always planned for me.

In John 8:32 the Bible says, *"You will know the truth and the truth will set you free"*. Isn't that what we all want: to be free? Isn't it the cry of every heart to walk in the freedom that God intended us to have from the start? Freedom comes from knowing the truth. And I believe that knowing the truth does not mean knowing **about** the truth. If it did, I would never have struggled with shame, for I know a great deal of truth. ***"Knowing"*** the truth is to rest in it, to bank on it, to trust it. It is choosing to live in what is real.

What is the truth? In what do we need to rest? What will set us free to be all that God created us to be?

The truth is that the God who created the universe is absolutely wild about you. God is so crazy in love with you—just as you are. His love for you reaches beyond any limit or boundary. His love has no breaking point. There is nothing you could do that would make Him love you any more than He does right now in this moment, and there is nothing you could do to make Him love you any less. His love for you is not dependent on you. You cannot earn God's love. It simply is. You cannot lose God's love because you did not earn it. It simply is.

You were God's idea from the start. He created you in His image and chose you before the foundation of the world. (Ephesians 1:4-6) One of the phrases in these verses does not usually get the attention it deserves. Not only did God choose us to be adopted as His children before the foundation of the world, but also, He chose us *"according with His pleasure and will"*. We were God's idea. And God does not make anything that is defective, worthless, wasteful or unacceptable. He is God and all that He has made is GOOD! Did He make you? Then, you are good!

Sometimes things are so obvious that they get unnoticed. I know about the father/child relationship for I am the child of my father. But one of the facts about being a child is that a person could never be the child of someone unless he has a father. No one on earth got here without a father contributing to the process.

You may have had a father that was uninvolved in your life, but I assure you, you indeed have a biological father. You had absolutely nothing at all to do with your conception. In the same way, we have absolutely nothing to do with the fact that we are God's children. We are His kids because He is the Father. There is nothing we could ever do to earn that position. We are God's because He chose us. God Himself has qualified us to be His. (Colossians 1:12)

God made us in His own image. You and I are unique, once-in-forever expressions of God. A statement like that will smash with force against a shame grid. It totally goes against all of the messages you have received that tell you that there is something defective about you. But this truth is worth fighting for.

Brennan Manning, in his book, "The Signature of Jesus" puts it this way, *"We are called to listen to God's first word to us. The word is a gift of ourselves to ourselves; our existence, our nature, our personal history, our uniqueness, our identity. All that we have and are is one of the unique and never-to-be-repeated ways God has chosen to express Himself in space and time. Each of us, made in His image and likeness, is yet another promise He has made to the universe that He will continue to love it and care for it."* (Multinoma Books, 1996) What an amazing thought! God has chosen to express Himself through us.

Part of the essence of shame is that it forces behavior and is an exercise of power over another. It is a way to control, a way to coerce. God could have chosen to exercise His power over us and force us to love Him.

If you look back into the Old Testament, there are several instances where God completely wiped out people who would not obey Him. The fate of Sodom and Gomorrah shows a God whose patience had run out. He destroyed all of those who lived there for their sin and disobedience, and then turned Lot's wife into a pillar of salt because she looked back when God had told her not to.

There is also the story of Noah. Only he and his family were saved from a worldwide flood that God sent to destroy everyone on earth because of their sin and disobedience. This is a powerful, mighty God whose glory was far too intense for Moses to see when he was on the mountain. He could only see where it had been, or he would have fallen dead from its power.

God could have chosen to use His power, but He didn't. God chose rather, to lay aside His power and to sacrifice the final Lamb, Jesus, to cover all of our sins once and for all. He laid aside His power for the love of us. He doesn't want our external performance; He wants our hearts. God has chosen to court us and romance us. He wants to dance with us. He wants to woo our hearts. God's power wouldn't help us; it was rather the laying aside of His power.

When Jesus is talking to His disciples in John 15, He says that He is "the vine", and we (the disciples) are "the branches". Have you ever seen a vine? Have you ever tried to untangle a vine? Vines are the most intimate of all plants. As they grow, they weave all around, over and under themselves. Jesus, by this example, is communicating relationship with His disciples. Not just any relationship, but an intimate relationship—the most intimate of relationships.

God created us to be in relationship with Him. From the creation of the world, man was God's idea, and man was created for God. The choice Adam and Eve made in the garden severed that relationship, and from that moment on, all of history has been about God pursuing us to restore that relationship. He relentlessly pursues us every moment of every day because He doesn't want to live without us.

Spending times of stillness and simply communing with Him will help you see that more clearly. Look for it. Listen for it. Expect it. God is wild about you!

Until about a hundred and seventy years ago, the term "born again" was seldom used. We know it today to mean that a person has gotten saved or has come into a personal relationship with Jesus. We see the term used in the story of

Jesus and Nicodemus in John 3 where Jesus tells Nicodemus in verse 3 *"no one can see the kingdom of God unless he is born again"*. However, this term was not commonly used in church history.

We use it as almost cliché today, but historically, the phrase used to describe an encounter with Jesus was, *"I have been seized by the power of a great affection"*. What a beautiful picture—to be captured, gripped and absorbed by God's incredible love for us. ("Thoughts From My Spiritual Journey", Glenn Murray http://www.glennmurray.nccn. net/a_fresh_look_at_the_gospel s.htm)

The Almighty God of the universe laid aside His power that could have forced us to love Him. He chose rather to romance us with His boundless love and amazing grace. He came to earth in the most humble manner, lived a simple life, and carried all of our shame and sin on his back as He hung naked, exposed and vulnerable on a cross.

I was preparing to share some comments before we observed Communion together as a church several years ago and I was captivated in a fresh way by the story of the cross. Jesus told us that He and the Father are one, and that if we have seen Him, we have seen the Father.

It dawned on me as if for the first time that this was God Himself who placed Himself willingly on that cross. This was a naked, exposed, humiliated God who experienced a vulnerability that we will never know. He not only was vulnerable physically, but He was also vulnerable in that He knew by choosing love over power, we would have the freedom to reject Him. He chose to take that risk.

What an amazing God! This is what God did for you. He is crazy about you. Shame has no place in the Christian experience. God has already sealed your eternal state of love, value and acceptance.

Fight for the faith to believe this truth. We already have what we so desperately want. God has sealed us with all that He has done, and our performance will not affect, change, add or remove it in any way. All that we have and all that we are is because God is God. Fight to rest in what God has done. *"Be transformed by the renewing of your mind"*, or as it reads in The Message, *"fix your attention on God. You'll be changed from the inside out."* Sounds a little bit like metamorphosis, doesn't it?

THE JOURNEY

The process of walking out of shame and into freedom takes
time. I did not arrive where I am today overnight, nor have
I yet finished the course. None of us will be perfected until
we reach heaven, so we are all in the process of "becoming."
At times, the progress may seem slow, and other times, it
may seem very quick. The point is that we are never static.
God is always at work even if we cannot feel it.

My journey has been a process of continual, steady growth, but it is not of my own effort, other than the fight to believe the truth and the fight to rest in it. The process began for me in the summer of 2002 when I sat in that breakout session and someone put words on my struggle.

For the first time, I was offered hope. The information was so liberating that it rocked my world. I was catapulted into a newfound freedom. It was as if I had gotten saved all over again—a second conversion experience. But then, I began to settle back into some old patterns, habits and reactions.

My encounter with God that one afternoon on Kennesaw Mountain was yet another marker moment in my journey. One more layer had come off, as if peeling an onion. My footing became sure again and I was walking in freedom. But the transformation was not complete. Once again, I found myself drifting back into some old patterns and habits. It was frustrating because I thought I knew better and that I was beyond this.

I am a fan of Pixar, the animation company partnered with Disney that made several animated films including the "Toy Story" trilogy, "A Bug's Life", "Monsters, Inc." My ultimate favorite is, "Finding Nemo." I can watch it over and over and never tire of it.

In November of 2004, Pixar released, "The Incredibles". In this movie about the mundane lives of a household full of superheroes forced into hiding, there is a scene where Bob Parr, a.k.a. "Mr. Incredible" has torn his super suit and has taken it to his clothing designer, Edna Mode, to be repaired.

Edna is eccentric and loud, and takes command of situations despite her small stature. In one particular scene, Edna makes a rather poignant statement when she says to Mr. Incredible, "I never look back, [dahling], it detracts from the now." The comment struck me as being quite true, looking back can indeed detract from the now. However sometimes it is good to look back. It might even be necessary. I have found this true in my journey.

In my days of hiking the mountain, I would sometimes have a friend with me who did not walk as often as I did, and for whom the climb was more difficult. Kennesaw Mountain actually is comprised of two peaks, and the more strenuous hike, ironically, is actually up the shorter hill.

My friend and I would usually just go to the top of the smaller peak and then turn around and return to the bottom. One morning, feeling a bit ambitious, we decided to continue over the top of the one and on to the larger summit. It was a hard hike, and it felt as if we would never make it up to the second peak. We stopped for a quick breather and I told my friend to look back and see how far we had come.

It was a moment to savor all of the ground we had covered, and it gave us motivation to continue the climb. Looking back reminded us of where we had been, but also gave us the opportunity to see how far we had come. It gave us what we needed to press on.

In my journey, it has been important to me to take a quick glance back every now and again and remember that I am not where I started. I will never go back to the bondage I knew for so long. I know too much, and God has been consistently revealing Himself to me, continuing to woo my heart with His love, His mercy and His grace. It takes time, but progress is sure. I can see how far I have come and I will never return from whence I came.

I bought a birthday card for a friend a few years ago. It was one of those "Good Shepherd" cards with the cute woolly sheep on it made by DaySpring Cards in Siloam Springs, Arkansas.

This card struck me with such significance that I bought a second one for myself. I brought it home and taped it to my bathroom mirror so that I would be continually reminded of things I have spent most of my life knowing but never really *knowing* to the point where I truly believed them.

The card has a sheep at the top that says, "Just wanted to share what the Shepherd has promised you for your birthday". When you unfold it lengthwise, it continues " ... and every other day of the life He's given you!"

Down the entire length of the card is a long, unwound scroll with several statements of truth written on it. They are specific tidbits from Scripture that communicate what God says about me. It tells me that I am God's child and that my times are in His hands. It reminds me that His thoughts toward me are precious and that He loves me with an everlasting love. He has promised to bless me. He has placed His hand on me and He holds me safely. He does everything for me in love because He is FOR me. He won't fail me.

Some of the truths in this card were harder for me to swallow than others. The thought of God being FOR me had always been so far beyond my perspective. God had never been represented as being "for me" before. I was convinced that He was out to get me. And I never really believed that His thoughts toward me were precious (Psalm 139). But truth is truth no matter what, and I have chosen to fight for the faith to believe it.

The process takes time. For someone who has lived a life conditioned to perform, behave and edit, it can be frustrating. Patience has never been my strong suit. But the more you work for acceptance and value, the more it will elude you. It is like trying to settle ripples in a pond. It is impossible to make the water surface smooth without causing more ripples. The water must be allowed simply to settle.

The more we try to perform our way out of shame, the more ripples we will cause. Let God do what He's doing and fight to rest in His performance rather than trying to earn what you already have. Learn to be still. Learn to rest in being God's beloved. He will complete the work He has started.

On yet another hike on the mountain, I was struggling with a decision that I needed to make. It was something that I didn't want to do, but something I had a hunch that God wanted me to do. I was fighting it out with Him on the mountain, again desperate to hear Him speak. He did.

Just as I was returning back down the mountain, seven beautiful black and royal blue butterflies crossed the path in front of me. I had never seen butterflies that color before. They were brilliant, and there were seven, a number with great significance in the Scriptures. God spoke clearly, almost audibly, as He tends to do with me on the mountain. He said, "You ARE a butterfly. You can't put yourself back into the bondage of the cocoon. It's too late for that." There was no room for argument at that point. It was clear, and I made the choice He wanted me to make. Those words have stuck with me. "You are a butterfly".

"It is for freedom that Christ has set you free." (Galatians 5:1 NIV) *"Christ has set us free to live a free life. So take your stand! Never again let anyone put a harness of slavery on you."* (The Message)

Fight to believe what is true because of what God has done—not because of any effort of your own. Fight to live in the truth that you are already loved, accepted, valued and that you are not alone. Fight to rest in what God has already done, what He continues to do, and what He will complete in your life.

God, Who began this work in you, will be faithful to complete it (Philippians 1:6). That is His promise. I marvel at where I stand now in this place in my life. God has done an amazing work in me, and I know He will complete it. I in no way believe that I have arrived. I still have my struggles, but I also know that I am not where I have been, nor will I ever return to that place. I know too much and I have tasted freedom.

Just like a butterfly that can never return to the cocoon, so will I never go back. I do not want to go back, and although I may wobble here and there, I know that God is at work.

I love the prayer of the Apostle Paul for the Ephesians in chapter 3, verses 16-19, *"I ask [the Father] to strengthen you by his Spirit—not a brute strength but a glorious inner strength—that Christ will live in you as you open the door and invite him in. And I ask him that with both feet planted firmly on love, you'll be able to take in with all followers of Jesus the extravagant dimensions of Christ's love. Reach out and experience the breadth! Test its length! Plumb the depths! Rise to the heights! Live full lives, full in the fullness of God"* (The Message).

It is also my prayer for all of you who read this, that you will be able to take it all in and that you will live full lives in the freedom that God intended. May you be "seized by the power of a great affection."

THE CAUTION

I have had the opportunity to share my story to several different groups over the past couple of years and I have found that the problem of shame is more widespread than I ever imagined. Some people have suggested that it is a universal predicament to some degree.

For years, I thought I was alone in my struggle. Now, I am not only walking in freedom, but I have also had the privilege of helping others into that same freedom. I have watched God put the key into the lock of shame and have seen chains fall to the ground as people realize that there is hope. The transformation process is absolutely amazing. But I believe that this book would be incomplete without addressing one final thought: forgiveness.

FORGIVING YOURSELF

Those who struggle with shame tend to be extremely hard on themselves. They believe that they can never measure up. There is no grace for their mistakes and they stand in their own judgment.

For me, I ended up in a place where I hated being in my own skin. I was so entrenched in the muck and mire of shame that all I wanted to do was to disappear. I could not receive the love and support I desperately wanted, and basically, I was starving to death. My life was in a downward spiral of desperation, hopelessness and defeat, and I was hurting those around me in the process.

When I sat in that breakout session in July of 2002, one of the things that the speaker addressed was this issue of self—hatred. I had never had those words put on it before, but when she said it, I knew I was guilty of it. I hated being me. It was that simple. There was very little about myself that I liked.

I was convinced that I was a complete failure. Like the Apostle Paul, I did things I didn't want to do and didn't do things that I wanted to do. I was a mess.

Shame leads to self-hatred, and self-hatred, in the most technical sense, is idolatry. It is a preoccupation with you. When you hate yourself, you are placing yourself at the center of your focus, not God. This is sin and we have to recognize it and repent.

God is not shocked when we fail. He knows that we are human. His opinion of us is not affected by whether or not we blow it. It has no bearing on our performance. His love is beyond boundary, limit or breaking point. He loves us as we are. He bought us in "as is" condition. None of us will ever be all that we are supposed to be this side of heaven, but God loves us as we are. He has forgiven all of our sins, even those we have not yet committed. How dare we not forgive ourselves?

In the book, "Posers, Fakers and Wannabe's", Brennan Manning writes the most amazing quote. It is so poignant and full of truth. It really captures the essence of the point I am trying to make and the need to forgive yourself.

*"God, who spoke us into existence, speaks to us now: 'Come out of self-hatred into my love. Come to me now,' he says. 'Forget about yourself. Accept who I long to be for you, who I am for you—your Rescuer—endlessly loving, forever patient, unbearably forgiving. Stop projecting your sick feelings onto me. You are a broken flower—I will not crush you—a flickering candle—I will not extinguish you. **For once and forever, relax: of all places, you are safe with me.**"'* (p. 26, emphasis added).

What a beautiful picture! Stop beating yourself up. Stop projecting your own sick feelings onto God. You are safe with Him.

FORGIVING OTHERS
If you have been a part of a system that has communicated shaming messages to you, chances are, you are feeling

wounded, rejected and ripped off, especially if you are looking back from a more healthy perspective. People that you were supposed to feel safe with were not available to you either physically or emotionally. Those in your life who should have provided a sense of well-being and safety, instead tore you down and crushed your spirit.

Perhaps you were physically abused. Maybe your mom or dad deserted you. Maybe your church twisted your view of God to the point that you wanted nothing to do with Him. Whatever your story, there are undoubtedly people in your life who have hurt you. Forgiveness must be found here as well. You have to make the choice to forgive those who have hurt you.

This is not easy. In fact, forgiving those who have wounded you may be one of the hardest choices you ever make. The problem with choosing not to forgive is that it holds you captive. You can spend your entire life laying blame and holding bitterness in your heart, but you end up being the only one affected by it. I have heard an example of this as pouring a cup of poison for your enemy, then drinking it yourself. Only you can consume the cup of your own bitterness.

I know a woman who is in her early 50's who has struggled with shame issues her entire life. Not only did she grew up in a family that is very dysfunctional and expert at sending shaming messages, but she was also part of a church environment that was very legalistic and focused on a list of do's and don'ts, rather than on the love and grace of God. Today, she spends a great deal of energy trying to figure out why she does what she does, why she reacts the way she reacts and why things affect her the way they do. This is valid, and there is great healing that comes from understanding your history and filling in the blanks, but at some point, you have to deal honestly with your own behavior.

This is a wife and mother of two children who is still stuck as a child in those shaming systems because she spends her energy completely focused on who has wronged her, and holding everyone else responsible for what she does today.

She will call members of her family and ask what it is that either her mother or her father did that causes her to struggle with whatever her struggle is at that moment. Rather than taking responsibility as an adult who has choices, she is still stuck in the blame game, looking at everyone else to be the cause of her struggle. She does not look honestly at her own choices. She has never fully forgiven her parents. She has never forgiven the church. She continues to hold them responsible for her actions, and consequently, she remains in the bondage of her own unforgiveness.

We have all been forgiven so much. There is not a single person who does not need God's mercy. The playing field is level in God's eyes. The Bible is full of verses dealing with forgiveness. We are told to forgive others as Christ has forgiven us. We are also told that if we do not forgive the sins of others against us, that God will in turn not forgive us. (Matthew 6)

Colossians 3:13 says *"Bear with each other and forgive whatever grievances you may have against one another. Forgive as the Lord forgave you."* Forgiveness is non-negotiable. It is a command.

Jesus suffered more humiliation, rejection, misunderstanding, judgment and wounding than we will ever experience in our lifetime. Nothing we experience will ever come close to what He chose to bear for us. While enduring the agony of the Cross, in His last breath, Jesus asked His Father to *"forgive them, for they do not know what they are doing"* (Luke 23:34).

He has forgiven us completely. How can we dare not forgive others?

FORGIVING GOD

I was talking to a pastor a while ago about the opportunities that I have had to share my story and to speak on shame. I mentioned to him that I had only just added a section at the end of my teaching that dealt with forgiveness and he agreed with me that this is indeed a significant issue and that it needs to be addressed.

At the time we spoke, I had ended my words about forgiveness here: We need to forgive ourselves, and we need to forgive others. But this pastor pointed out that there is typically a third place where forgiveness should fall and it is often not addressed. It is the need to forgive God.

This may sound a bit bold on my part, but I believe that we as humans have the tendency to blame God. Maybe we're mad at Him for putting us in the family we were born into. Maybe we are disappointed in His timeframe or disillusioned when things don't work out the way we think they should. Maybe we are frustrated when doors remain closed that we think should be opened. Maybe God has let us down. Maybe.

Maybe it's just me, but I think we all have had our issues with God. Although the idea of forgiving God could become a book in itself, I will only touch on a few things here that I think are paramount.

God's heart is for us. Whether or not we choose to believe It will not change the fact that it is. We know that God is good, but do we really believe that His heart is for us? Do we really accept as true that He can be trusted? We have to start here. Unless we choose to believe that God loves us and that He is for us, we will never truly have peace. He is good all the time, whether we feel it or not. He cannot make mistakes and He cannot fail.

I will never begin to understand God. He is far too big for my frail, human mind to wrap around. But I have seen it proven over and over again that He is faithful, and that He never wastes anything, no matter what we may endure here on earth.

A very dear friend of mine moved with her family from Chicago to the Atlanta area in 1997 after her husband took a new job. Within a week after starting his position he was injured. He spent the next seven years primarily in bed with severe, debilitating back pain. The injury was such that no surgeon wanted to risk touching him, so the quest to rid him of pain became a journey of attempting to manage his pain.

Very early on, while having a quiet time with the Lord, my friend found herself at a place with God where He basically laid it out on the table. He said to her that morning, "Either I'm Lord or I'm not." There was no middle ground. She had to choose right there, not knowing what the following years would hold for her and her family. That day, she covenanted with God that she would trust Him as sovereign. She chose to trust Him as Lord.

Several years later, a new doctor re-evaluated his case and new technology was available. He ended up having surgery to repair the damage in his back and it was very successful. After a horrible season of rehabilitation and withdrawal from pain medication, he began to re-engage in his life. Their children had their father back. My friend had her husband back. Things seemed to be getting back on track.

He began pursuing some schooling to get new skills for a home-based guitar building and repair business. The future seemed to be full of hope and promise, but a reckless driver stole that dream. He was hit head on while driving home from school just two and a half weeks after classes had begun. He was killed instantly.

This does not make sense. It will never make sense. If anyone has a reason to blame God, it is my friend who had already walked an incredibly painful, difficult road only to have a brief taste of redemption for all of the time lost and then lose it again forever. But even in the midst of her grief and loss, she continues to go back to that covenant made with God several years earlier. "Either I'm Lord, or I'm not."

As for my friend, she will always have hope (Psalm 71:14). She has chosen to trust God's heart as good, even though she will never understand why this tragedy happened.

As senseless as this may seem, God has not wasted any of it. And although all of us who knew him are all still reeling from the impact of this loss, we have to trust that God is good and that it is His nature to restore.

Look at Job who lost everything and suffered emotional pain that many of us will never know. We can look back from our perspective now knowing the outcome of the story and knowing that all he had lost was restored to him seven-fold. Job, however, didn't know what was to come. All he knew was his loss, his grief and his pain. Still he chose to trust God's heart for him. He chose to trust that God was good, even in the middle of his suffering. Job stands as God's witness that He will restore.

Be careful to keep short accounts in these areas. Choose to forgive yourself. Don't be your own judge and jury. Realize that God loves you and no matter what you have done, His blood covers you and your slate is clean before Him.

Choose to forgive others for the wounds their actions or words may have caused you. We are all in need of God's mercy and we have all been forgiven much. Holding bitterness and anger toward your brother only affects you.

Finally, choose to rest in the truth that God is sovereign. He does not make mistakes. Trust Him with your circumstances, trust Him with your past, trust Him with your future and trust Him with your pain. Either He is Lord or He is not. You decide.

THE HOPE

One chilly night, a friend of mine fell asleep in her living room while enjoying a nice, warm fire in her fireplace. When she awoke the next morning, the fire had been reduced to a quiet pile of ash, only a memory of the raging flames from the night before. As she looked more closely into the ashes, she saw a tiny flicker of an ember that was still aglow. Under the right circumstances that one little ember could once again become a hot, fiery blaze.

In the middle of what seemed like a dead pile of ash, there was indeed life. There was potential. There was hope for a fire to burn once again.

Maybe you have spent your life yielding to the burden of shame because you have worn it so long. It has become familiar. It has become comfortable. It is all you have known.

It has become your "normal" and perhaps you feel as if there is no chance that you will ever be free from it. Maybe you need to fight for the "want to," or the desire to be free.

Don't give up. Where there is life, there is hope. Things do not have be the way they have always been. God is bigger than anything you have ever, or will ever encounter. No matter how cold and lifeless the ashes appear, there is always a spark of potential hidden, waiting for someone or something to come along and fan the flame. It is my prayer that my story will help fan that flame, no matter how dim it may be.

Just as the caterpillar quiets himself in complete rest inside that cocoon, quiet yourself in the certainty of God's work in your life. Often we forget that all that we know, all that we see and all that we experience is not all that there is. There is much going on behind the scenes and beneath the surface. God is at work. There is a butterfly forming and one day it will begin to stir. New life will awaken, wings will unfold and a butterfly will be born.

EPILOGUE

I do not think of myself as being an authority on the subject of shame, nor am I completely free from the impact of the shaming messages received in my past. I do know that I am not where I was, nor am I where I will end up. Life is a journey and I cannot go back.

Writing this book was not fun or easy because the enemy used every opportunity he could find to push my shame buttons. He tried to convince me that I have no right to speak these truths to others when I still struggle with them myself.

Someone told me early on that as I wrote the book, the book would write me—and it has. I am farther along in my journey than I was when I began writing. I have been obedient to what I believe God called me to do and if God speaks to you through me sharing my story then I am humbled and honored. He speaks in spite of me, and it is all for His glory.

May God bless you on your journey. In the name of Jesus, who came to bring true freedom: May shame on you NO MORE!

ILLUSTRATOR'S NOTES
By Claire "Vimala" Anderson

It is more than just a privilege; it is a Grace to be able to share these images with you in this particular volume.

Cathy Little is someone I have known and loved throughout my life. I met her in the garage at my childhood home when she arrived home at little more than two weeks old. I was ten and a half years old and for all intents and purposes, she became my real life baby doll. She is my sister. I have watched her grow in wisdom and stature throughout the years and can say that it is a joy and a delight to have her in my life.

When Cass [that's who she *really* is] asked me to consider this project, she gave me free reign in the selection process. She trusted me and I hope I have not let her down. I would like to open a small doorway into my process in making the choices I did. More often than not, it was not until after the image came to mind that I saw in retrospect how perfect the choice was. It also let me know that this project was far bigger than she or I, and that we were merely two players in a much larger and Divine cast. Perhaps you too will see …

The Cover … *Butterfly on a flower.* This little guy was the last in a long line of butterflies that came out to be photographed one afternoon as I was walking. Cass had suggested the possibility of me illustrating her book earlier and I knew that the butterfly was a significant archetype in her manuscript. I had commented to her that I didn't have any butterfly photos as they were all so fluttery and wouldn't hold still. That afternoon, I knew something was up, as a veritable army of butterflies deliberately placed themselves in my camera's view. The first ones were a bit rough looking. All beat up with tears in their wings or small chunks missing. Yet they seemed more than willing to show off their remaining beauty. As I walked further, each one became more and more whole and perfect in form. Our cover model was the crowning glory of the whole afternoon. A testimony to the beauty in us all waiting to be rediscovered.

Introduction … *Apple blossoms.* In the beginning of her writing process, she is unsure, but encouraged and determined to write. The project is in blossom and in many ways, so is she.

The Problem … *A butterfly on a rusty old bridge.* All that fresh beauty sits on something old and past it's prime, perhaps past it's usefulness. And it waits there contemplating, like it's ready for an explanation, waiting for something new.

The Message … *The tree reflected on water.* This is shame. We are perfectly fine trees, but we see ourselves upside down in a mud puddle. It's just a matter of perspective but it can be crippling as we see in the next image … *[Interestingly, this photo was taken in our hometown where much of the story takes place.]*

The Impact … *The shaky tree.* There's that tree, right-side up and in the real world yet it's all shaken up.

The Grid ... *Prison bars*. I took this photo in Montreux, Switzerland at the Castle Chillon. It housed many famous and infamous prisoners in its day. Their only view of freedom was through these bars as they passed by this doorway and into the dungeon.

The Cycle ... *A millstone*. This seemed a fitting illustration of the repeating cycle of shame. Used for grinding grain into flour, it did its work of breaking the seeds down, a form of destruction and yet making the grain more useful. In the end the wheel itself is worn down and cast away. Cycles for everything.

The Process ... *A black butterfly on a thorny thistle*. Cass uses the idea of metamorphosis with great effectiveness. There is a beginning, a middle, and an ending. Nothing gets skipped. This little guy has made it to adulthood and he seems to tell us all to maintain. Everything is working itself out. Flight is eminent!

The Fight ... *Flowers hanging on in the rushing water*. I took this photo in March at a Pennsylvania state park. These Queen Ann's Lace had held on throughout the winter storms and early spring rains at the edge of the Mill's spillway and never let go. They are an inspiration and example of perseverance.

The Truth ... *A rock*. Cath writes that when the reality of who she is came to her, it was as solid as the rocks beneath her feet. This photo stands in for all rocks, with its many layers. It is sure. It is real. It is forever.

The Journey ... *A riverside path*. Solid trees line the path. It's not necessarily level or paved but it's well-marked. And it leads us somewhere ... when we take the steps.

The Caution ... *A life preserver for emergency use.* Just the sight of the life preserver will clue hikers to the possibility of hazards along the way. There is also a sense of security in knowing they are there, if we do happen to fall into the waters of life.

The Hope ... *The sun shining through after a rain.* The sun peeked out after one of those intense days filled with storms, watches and warnings. It peeked out as if nothing had ever happened. Oblivious to the stress we had all been under. The sun is constant. Always there. Shining away whether we see it or not. That's hope.

Epilogue ... *Green apples from the same tree.* Remember the blossoms? The book is now done. When she finishes, the process itself has done a work in her. She is not where she was, yet not where she will be either. So the apples are green. No longer blossoms, but not fully ripe. Like most of us, eh?

"STONES OF REMEMBRANCE"

As humans, we often need to be reminded of things. We are forgetful. That is why God on many occasions called His people to set up reminders so that they would not forget what He had done for them.

In Joshua 4, we read the story of the Children of Israel crossing the River Jordan on dry ground. God told them to set up twelve stones where the river had parted, one for each of the twelve tribes of Judah, as a permanent reminder of what God had done there that day.

In the Upper Room, just before His arrest and crucifixion, Jesus established "The Lord's Supper", or "Communion" as we call it today. This was instituted as a reminder of what Jesus was about do to. We observe it to bring us back to the finished work of Christ for us, forever sealing our eternal state of acceptance by the Father. Every time we take the bread and the cup, we are reminded of the body that was broken and blood that was poured out for us.

In May of 2006, I decided to celebrate what God had been doing in my life with my own "Stone of Remembrance". I got a tattoo. Not just any tattoo, but a tattoo of spiritual significance. And I did not get one just for the sake of getting one, but rather for the sake of permanently reminding me that I am no longer what I was.

I have a tribal butterfly tattooed on my right shoulder. It reminds me that I am no longer crawling on the ground, but I am a butterfly with wings to fly. When I am tempted to doubt the work of God in my life, or when the enemy challenges me, I can look at that tattoo and I can see the branding of the Father and it says to me, "I am forever His."

I can say with confidence that I *was* enslaved by shame ... **but now**; I am walking in the freedom God designed me to know.

AFTERWARDS

I finished writing this book in March of 2007. Little did I know what lay before me. The layer of healing documented in this book is not a finished work; it is rather a necessary beginning to something much deeper.

In the summer of 2008, God allowed some things to be exposed in my life. There were still areas that He wanted access to, places that needed healing and wholeness. What happened to trigger Phase 2 of my healing is one of the darkest, most forgettable moments of my life.

My mantra through the journey has been that I would not wish my circumstances on anyone, but I would not trade what God has done through them for anything. The process nearly killed me. Literally. Yet, the healing and wholeness I have come to know on this side is proof that God does work all things together for good (Romans 8:28).

I stand on this side of what I now see as a two-part healing. The layer of healing that God did in my life regarding shame was critical to the finishing work He began that summer. Without the certainty of God's love for me regardless of anything I had ever done or could ever do, I can pretty much guarantee you that I would not be alive right now.

In the wake of my personal "crash and burn," I knew that God still loved me just as much as He ever had. I knew that my failure was powerless to change that fact. I knew that He looked beyond my behavior, my choices, my sin, and He saw me in the fullness of the potential and destiny for which He had created me.

There will be another book some day, one that provides the other bookend to my journey, but today is not that day. For now, Part 2 is currently documented in a 5 song EP called, "*Safely Through.*" For more information on the EP, go to www.simply-worship.org.

ABOUT THE AUTHOR

Cathy has been involved in leading worship for over two decades. She is the founder and director of www.Simply-Worship.org, a nonprofit ministry dedicated to developing great worship leaders from the inside out. Through teaching, consulting and one-on-one coaching, Cathy addresses the heart issues of character, authenticity and integrity. She also provides practical tools for effective and skillful worship leadership.

Originally from Pennsylvania, Cathy moved to the Atlanta, GA area in 1993 where she continues to serve in her local church and do ministry wherever God opens a door.

SUGGESTED RESOURCES:

Jeff VanVonderen, *Tired of Trying to Measure Up*, (Bethany House Publishers, 1989)

David Johnson and Jeff VanVonderen, *The Subtle Power of Spiritual Abuse*, (Bethany House Publishers, 1991)

William Backus and Marie Chapian, *Telling Yourself The Truth*, (Bethany House Publishers, 1980)

Brennan Manning, *The Signature of Jesus*, (Multnomah Publishers Inc., 1988,1992,1996)

Brennan Manning, *The Ragamuffin Gospel*, (Multnomah Publishers, Inc., 1990, 2000)

Rob Bell, *Velvet Elvis: Repainting the Christian Faith*, (Zondervan, 2005)

Brennan Manning and Jim Hancock, *Posers, Fakers and Wannabe's: Unmasking the Real You"* (Navpress, 2003)

Jarrett Stevens, *The Deity Formerly Known As God*, (Zondervan, 2006)